Working Together Against
GUN VIOLENCE

After her husband and son were victims of gun violence, Carolyn McCarthy worked to support gun control laws by becoming a representative in Congress.

Working Together Against

GUN VIOLENCE

Maryann Miller

THE ROSEN PUBLISHING GROUP, INC.
NEW YORK

Published in 1994, 1997 by The Rosen Publishing Group, Inc.
29 East 21st Street, New York, NY 10010

Copyright 1994, 1997 by The Rosen Publishing Group, Inc.

Revised Edition 1997

Library of Congress Cataloging-in-Publication Data

Miller, Maryann, 1943–
    Working together against gun violence / Maryann Miller.
        p.   cm. — (The Library of social activism)
    Includes bibliographical references and index.
    ISBN 0-8239-2612-5
    1. Gun control—United States—Juvenile literature.   2. Violence—
United States—Juvenile literature.   3. Youth volunteers in social
service—United States—Juvenile literature.   [1. Gun control.
2. Violence.   3. Social action.]   I. Title.   II. Series.
HV7436.M55   1994
363.3′3′0973—dc20   94-1021
                                                                                    CIP
                                                                                    AC

Manufactured in the United States of America

Contents

INTRODUCTION

SOME EXPERTS HAVE SAID THAT WE ARE IN THE middle of an epidemic of gun violence. They mean that gun violence is increasing so rapidly that it is like the spread of a deadly disease. It is a major concern all over, in cities, suburbs, towns, and rural areas. The murder rate in Little Rock, Arkansas, is equal to that of New York City or Los Angeles.

The rising epidemic of gun violence has hit young people especially hard. More young people die from gun violence than from any other cause. Every two hours another American child is killed by a gun. More and more guns are finding their way into the hands of young people, with tragic results. All around us, children are killing and being killed.

The statistics may be bleak, but the situation is far from hopeless. There are ways that we all can contribute to ending the bloodshed. This book will help you learn about gun violence—what causes it and what we can do to stop it.

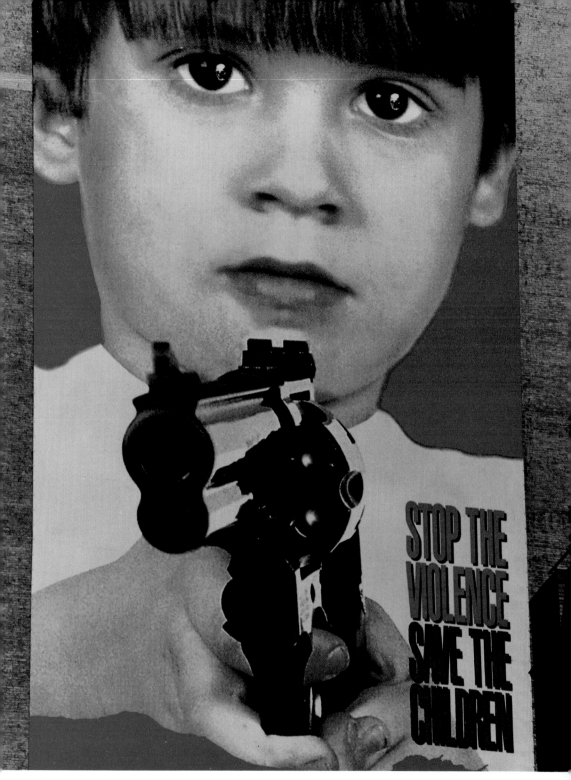

Gun violence among young people has become the subject of national attention.

Police arrived on the scene after a student shot two classmates at Thomas Jefferson High School in Brooklyn, New York.

chapter

1

LINKING GUNS AND VIOLENCE

IN THOMAS JEFFERSON HIGH SCHOOL IN New York City, there are six grieving rooms. Students go to these rooms when there is a shooting at school. There, they try to come to grips with the latest tragedy.

Schools should not need grieving rooms. They should not need metal detectors. Too many students go to school afraid of gun violence.

Carol A. Beck, the principal at Jefferson High in the borough of Brooklyn, is concerned. "Our last place of safety is the school," she says. "Next to Mother's arms, that should be the safest place."

Forty-seven states have passed mandatory suspension laws for students found with guns. Nonetheless, more than 100,000 students carry a gun to school every day. Some of these students are as young as nine years old.

In Chicago, weapons searches became part of a police project to stop gang and drug activity.

School officials do what they can to keep guns out. Many schools have metal detectors. Security guards patrol the halls. In some schools, students have safety drills for times when they hear gunfire in school.

These efforts are better than doing nothing. But they also create problems. The security disturbs the normal school routine. It also increases anxiety about safety.

Speaking of the students at Jefferson High, Ms. Beck says, "These children are children of war. They worry that in the blink of an eye they could be killed—this is a reality."

That reality should change. Parents, teachers, and students all agree that our schools should be safe.

❖ IN OUR HOMES ❖

Gun violence is also a problem in many neighborhoods. In some, armed gang members or drug dealers are on every corner. People are killed in drive-by shootings.

But gun violence doesn't just happen in the streets or between strangers. Most gun violence occurs in the home, where people are shot by their relatives and friends. A person who is depressed will be more likely to commit suicide when a gun is in his or her home. Some experts claim that having a gun in the house makes it three times more likely that someone will be murdered there.

❖ FACTS TO CONSIDER ❖

The leading cause of death among teenagers is from gunshot wounds. Nationwide, fifteen teens are killed by guns each day. Some are killed by accident. Some are deliberately shot. The rest are victims of suicide. Particularly in poor neighborhoods and housing projects, gun violence is the leading cause of death among African Americans between fifteen and twenty-four years old.

In 1994, guns were used to kill 38,505 people in the United States. Almost 31 percent of these victims were under twenty-four years old. Of the total number of gun-related deaths, 17,866 were murders and 18,765 were suicides. Guns were also used in more than one million crimes that year.

In a two-year period, more Americans were killed by guns in the United States than were killed in the entire Vietnam War.

Between 200 million and 250 million guns are owned by civilians in the United States. From 1985 to 1994, the FBI received an average of 274,000 reports of stolen guns every year. Every stolen gun is a gun that is available to criminals.

❖ HOLDING THE GUN ❖

Young people are not only victims of gun violence. They are also causing it. Even though it is illegal for anyone under eighteen to own a gun, murders committed by young people with firearms have nearly tripled since 1985.

People are also using guns at younger ages. In February 1993, an eight-year-old boy was charged with aggravated assault and armed burglary in Florida. He stole guns from a neighbor's house. Then he threatened his seven-year-old friend.

Young people have also injured or killed others in gun accidents. This can happen when children are able to play with their parents' gun.

Some children learn about guns from what they see on television—they don't see the consequences. "In a shooting there are always two victims," says Dr. Robert Lawrence. "The one who gets shot and the one who does the shooting."

The shooting of two students at Thomas Jefferson High School united the community against gun violence.

But too many young people don't realize that before they use a gun. One fifteen-year-old boy shot a man during a robbery at a gas station. The police found him staring at the man he had shot, too upset to run. At his trial, his mother said he was shocked at what he had done.

❖ QUESTIONS TO ASK YOURSELF ❖

Gun violence affects many communities—from big cities to small towns. Let's think about how it might affect you. 1) Do you feel that your school is a safe place? Why or why not? 2) How do you feel about teens your age or younger carrying guns?

13

chapter

2

UNDERLYING CAUSES

"**I** WISH THEY'D JUST GET RID OF ALL THE GUNS," said one teenager. "Pick them all up and throw them away." It would be nice to have such a simple solution. But the problem of gun violence is not just the guns. It's the people who use them and how they are used.

In a perfect world, guns would be used safely and only by licensed hunters and sports enthusiasts. Guns would never be in the hands of criminals or children.

In a perfect world, there would be no drugs or gangs terrorizing schools and neighborhoods. There would be no violence in homes, with family members being beaten and killed.

We live in an imperfect world, however. In our world, people are using guns to kill each other at an alarming rate.

Too often, people are trying to settle their conflicts with guns. Conflicts can be related to problems in our society that are caused by poverty and

The mayor of Chicago closed a housing project after a sniper killed a seven-year-old boy.

drugs. At the same time, many people do not respect our laws against violence.

Many people agree that there is a feeling of lawlessness in the United States. Some social scientists are concerned about what they call a moral breakdown. Many people are not taking responsibility for their own behavior.

Cornel West, a professor at Princeton University, agrees. In his book *Race Matters*, he states that Americans are no longer "standing on firm moral ground."

We live in a society where many people do

15

not follow rules and laws. West talks about dishonesty: lying and cheating in business, school, and politics. "Because everyone is doing it, it appears to be okay. And that is the example we are giving our children."

❖ WHAT CAUSES VIOLENCE? ❖

Two problems that may contribute to violence are poverty and drugs.

Often, people who are poor feel frustrated and powerless. Sometimes these feelings turn into anger and rage. Out of that rage can come an urge to lash out at other people. If a gun is handy, the urge can be deadly.

There has always been a connection between violence and drugs. People using illegal drugs commit four to six times as many crimes as people who do not use drugs. Many gangs are also involved in drugs, and gang activity causes much of the violence on the streets.

In addition to drugs and poverty, many people believe that violence in entertainment contributes to the problem. Movies, television, and music frequently portray violence in an unrealistic way. Often, they do not show the consequences of gun violence. The people who use guns on television may seem cool or are considered heroes. Many experts believe that these images make people think that gun violence is normal and harmless.

Working to reduce these causes can help make people less violent. When a community is able to reduce its poverty or drug use, the number of gun deaths can drop. There have also been efforts to keep young children from seeing graphic violence on television.

Some people believe that this is not enough. There will always be conflicts. But when a gun is around, people are more likely to become violent. Some people also think that owning a gun can make someone more likely to start a fight with others.

These arguments are used to support the idea that guns are also part of the problem. People who agree with this idea believe that there will be less violence if there are fewer guns. They think that there should be stricter gun control laws that limit what kind of gun a person can buy and who can get one.

❖ QUESTIONS TO ASK YOURSELF ❖

The arguments for and against gun control are endless. Each side makes good points, and it is not an easy issue to decide. You should consider all the ideas and opinions, and decide for yourself.

At this point it might be good to talk about gun control with others. You could ask one of your teachers to make it a class discussion. Or you could get a group of friends together and talk informally.

Here are some questions to consider in your discussion:

1) Do you agree with the student who wants to get rid of all the guns? Why or why not?
2) Would gun control cut down the number of deaths due to guns? How?
3) Do you think violence in entertainment contributes to real-life violence?
4) Do you think people should have a clearer definition of right and wrong? Do you think it would help people behave better?
5) Should people be more responsible about guns without the government having to tell them?
6) If you had a gun would you take gun safety classes? Do you think everyone should?

chapter

3

DO WE NEED GUNS?

A MAN IN TEXAS WAS CELEBRATING THE ARRIVAL of 1997 by shooting off his pistol outside his house on New Year's Eve. When the gun jammed, he went inside to fix it. As he was trying to remove the bullet, the gun went off and shot his seven-year-old daughter in the chest. "Daddy, I'm okay," she said. Then she died in his arms.

Stories like this make some people wonder why we have guns. They really aren't as necessary as they once were.

Generations ago, people needed guns. Guns were used to hunt for food. They were used for protection against threats from the wilderness. A gun was as common in every home as a coffeepot.

It was also common for children to learn how to use guns properly. They understood when and how guns should be used and when they shouldn't.

Federal agents captured the weapons stockpile of an Idaho man after he shot a federal marshal in 1992.

Today, people don't use guns for the same reasons. Hunting has become a sport. Most of us don't need to be protected from the wilderness. We rely on the police to protect us from criminals.

People today don't have the same attitudes about guns. Many children see them as toys. Fewer people are trained to handle guns properly. And some people own a gun only for the feeling of power it gives them.

❖ GUN LAWS ❖

Guns have been regulated throughout the history of the United States. Before the American Revolutionary War, the Colony of Massachusetts passed a law forbidding people to carry weapons in public places. During the 1800s, many states passed laws against carrying concealed weapons. Today, many states allow or are considering allowing licenses for concealed weapons.

Other laws regulate where people can have guns and how they can be used. Can you carry a gun in your car? Can you carry one in a public place? Can you carry it on the street?

Some city and state laws control who may own a gun license. These laws try to keep guns away from people who have committed violent crimes in the past.

Gun laws are different in every city and state. This can cause problems. For example, it is illegal to buy a handgun in Washington, DC. Yet the number of gun-related crimes in the city is high because residents can buy guns in nearby states.

Many people agree that we need federal gun laws to govern everybody. In recent years, several important federal laws have been passed, including the Brady Law of 1993. The Brady Law requires a five-day waiting period to do a background check on people who apply to buy guns. People who are upset and impulsively buy a gun will be able to "cool off" during this time. The law was named for former Press Secretary James Brady, a presidential aide who was shot during an assassination attempt on President Ronald Reagan in 1981.

Another law was passed in 1994 that banned certain types of semiautomatic assault weapons. Although the House of Representatives voted to repeal the ban, the Senate took no action on it, and the ban still stands. In 1996 a law went into effect that prohibits persons convicted of any domestic violence crime from owning a gun. Gun control advocates support these federal laws, but say that even stricter ones are needed to stop the spread of gun violence.

❖ HANDGUN CONTROL, INC. ❖

After his son was shot and killed in 1974, Pete Shields joined the National Council to Control

Press Secretary James Brady was shot by a man attempting to kill
US President Ronald Reagan in 1981.

Handguns (NCCH). Shields wanted to do something positive.

In 1975, Shields started working full-time for gun control. NCCH changed its name to Handgun Control, Inc. It calls for new federal laws to keep handguns out of the wrong hands.

Some of the proposed laws include:

- a mandatory jail sentence for using a handgun while committing a crime;
- a license-to-carry law—a special license would be needed to carry a handgun outside a home or place of business;
- a ban on the manufacture and sale of snub-nosed handguns;
- a ban on the manufacture and sale of plastic handguns, which can get past metal detectors and other security screening devices;
- mandatory safety-training programs for people who buy handguns.

❖ QUESTIONS TO ASK YOURSELF ❖

Gun laws vary from city to city, state to state. Take a look at your community. 1) What are the gun laws in your city and state? 2) If you were in your local legislature, would you work to change any of these laws? If so, how?

chapter

4

THE GUN CONTROL DEBATE

PEOPLE AGREE THAT GUN VIOLENCE IS A serious problem. But they have different ideas about what should be done about it.

Many mental health professionals think we should have gun control. They say it would get *fast* results while solutions to the problems that cause violence are sought.

They also want laws to keep guns away from young people. "Both suicide and homicide are teens' expression of rage," says Dr. Ralph Gemeli of Children's Hospital in Washington, DC. "If a gun is not at hand, it will lessen the chance of dying."

Opponents of gun control say that this is not the solution. People will just find other ways of killing themselves and each other.

But we don't really know if gun control would work or not. Each statistic or study mentioned by a pro-gun control group is argued against by an anti-gun control group.

❖ GUN CONTROL IN OTHER COUNTRIES ❖

Canada, Switzerland, Great Britain, and many other countries have low rates of homicide by handguns. They also have strict handgun laws.

To own a handgun in those countries people have to have a license. Before they can get the license, they go through a long application process, including a background check. A person also has to show a good reason for wanting to own a gun. The reason can be hunting, collecting, or sport. Self-defense and the protection of property are not considered good reasons.

In Japan, the only people who can have handguns are government security officers and athletes in training for shooting events. Japan also has one of the lowest criminal violence rates of all countries.

People against gun control argue that the laws really don't make a difference. They say that there is less violence in other countries because the cultures are stricter. These people say there is a stronger sense of right and wrong, and they believe people are more responsible for their actions.

On the other hand, people are people, no matter where they live. They get mad at each other. They get into arguments and fights. But in other countries, it's harder to find a gun to shoot somebody.

Metal detectors and security guards at school are two methods of
increasing student safety.

Dr. Steven F. Messner is a homicide re-
searcher at the State University of New York in
Albany. He says, "Homicide is social behavior.
It's behavior that people can change and they
do change." He does not think gun control will
make that change, but it will keep some violence
from being lethal.

❖ THE SECOND AMENDMENT ❖

The strongest argument against gun control
is tied to the U.S. Constitution. Some people
believe the Second Amendment in the Bill of

27

Rights gives all Americans the right to own a gun.

> "A well regulated Militia being necessary to the security of a free State, the right of the people to keep and bear arms, shall not be infringed."

That Bill was written in 1791 and has been debated ever since. When it was written, America had only 14 states. Each state had its own militia, a citizen army. All the men in the state were part of the militia. They could be called upon to help protect the United States if necessary.

Nobody is sure exactly what the Bill means to us in today's world. Does the "right of the people to keep and bear arms" apply only to the militia? Some people think so. They believe that citizens who are not part of the militia have no right to own guns.

Other people say the "right to keep and bear arms" is separate from the militia. Any citizen can own a gun.

The Supreme Court is the highest authority on what our Constitution means. In 1876 the Supreme Court made its first Second Amendment decision. It said that, "The bearing of arms for a lawful purpose is not a right granted by the Constitution."

Despite the danger of guns, many people firmly support the right to possess weapons.

Three other cases have been decided by the Supreme Court since then, in 1886, in 1939, and in 1984. Since then, the Court has refused to rule on other gun control cases.

Gun control supporters believe that the Supreme Court has given a clear answer: Owning a gun is not a constitutional right.

Those against gun control reject that view. They believe that the Court's decisions do not permit the government to regulate all guns.

Some people don't think that the Constitution can tell us what we can or can't do in every situation. The Constitution cannot always help us to make moral decisions. We have to decide for ourselves what the right thing to do is.

We also have to consider the changes in society since the Bill of Rights was written. The people who wrote it never thought of gang shoot-outs or schools that would need metal detectors to keep guns out.

What was good in 1791 may not be good today.

❖ **QUESTIONS TO ASK YOURSELF** ❖

People have different opinions about gun control. Explore your own feelings about the issue. What do you interpret "the right of the people to bear arms" to mean?

chapter

5

THE CASE AGAINST GUN CONTROL

MANY PEOPLE OBJECT TO GUN CONTROL. THEY are worried that allowing the government to restrict guns will lead to a ban on guns in the future.

The most powerful group against gun control is the National Rifle Association (NRA). It was started in 1871 by officers of the National Guard. Its purpose then was to promote good marksmanship and safe gun ownership.

Today, the NRA has close to 3 million members, among them gun collectors, gun dealers, gun manufacturers, hunters, and sports shooters. It is the oldest sportsperson's organization in the country.

A staff of 350 NRA people work in Washington, DC, against gun control. They try to convince legislators to vote against gun control laws. This is called lobbying.

The NRA also supports political candidates who are against gun control and gives money to their campaigns. In 1994, the NRA spent over 5 million dollars to help elect candidates it supported.

Other organizations work against gun con-
trol: the Second Amendment Foundation, the
Citizens Committee for the Right to Keep and
Bear Arms, and Gun Owners of America.

Organizations against gun control are concerned about violent crime. They just don't
think gun control is the answer. They favor
stiff laws against gun-related crimes and better
enforcement of those laws.

The opponents of gun control contend that
most Americans don't favor gun control. They
believe that the laws we already have don't work.

❖ REASONS AGAINST GUN CONTROL ❖

One argument against gun control is self-
protection. Some people believe that having a
gun will make you safe. If someone breaks into
your house, you might scare him away with a
gun. If someone tries to mug you in the street,
you might save yourself with a gun.

One study shows that nearly 650,000 people
have used handguns for protection from criminals. More than 300,000 other people have used
rifles or other "long guns" for protection.

Another common belief is that having a gun
will turn some criminals away. In a study of
1,800 prisoners, two researchers found some
interesting results:

- 85 percent said that a smart criminal will
  find out if people are armed

- 75 percent believed that burglars passed occupied buildings by, for fear of being shot
- 53 percent did not carry out the crime for fear the victim was armed
- 57 percent were scared off or shot at by armed victims
- 60 percent think that most criminals are more afraid of being shot by citizens than by the police

Arguments are also made against the belief that gun control would reduce violence. Gun registration is one example. Prisoners say, "Gun laws only affect people who obey the law. Criminals will always be able to get guns."

People against gun control argue that gun laws won't reduce crime, either. Cities and states with strict control laws have seen no change in crime rates.

People who favor gun control say those reasons are not good enough. Guns bought for protection too often end up being used for something else.

- They are often stolen and used by criminals
- They are involved in accidents when children play with them
- They are used for suicide
- They are used in arguments to kill a family member

❖ YOU DECIDE ❖

It's difficult to decide who is right in the gun control debate. The information is sometimes confusing. We may be able to find some answers by learning from countries where gun violence is much less common. The following list compares the total number of people killed by handguns in the United States and three other countries in the same year.

Great Britain	22
Canada	68
Japan	87
United States	11,719

Whatever the answer may be, the rate of gun violence in the United States is a problem that needs our effort and attention.

❖ QUESTIONS TO ASK YOURSELF ❖

As you have seen, gun control is an important issue in our society. For years, gun control laws have brought about a lot of debate. The following two questions might help you decide what you think about the issue: 1) What reasons do most people you know give to support or oppose gun control? 2) You have seen the statistics on gun-related deaths in the United States. Do you think gun control would affect these numbers?

chapter

6

PEOPLE WHO ARE DOING SOMETHING

MICHAEL CARR IS AN ARTIST WHO LIVES IN Washington, D.C. In January 1992, he decided to make a vivid record of the number of homicides in the city. By December of that year he had drawn 452 silhouettes in an alley he calls the "Court of Sorrows." The silhouettes represent the men, women, and children who had been killed that year.

Sometimes it is too easy to forget about the victims of gun violence. Carr believes we shouldn't forget.

With the help of Police Sgt. Gerald Neill, Carr also paints silhouettes on canvas. In January 1993, he took some of those canvases to the Inaugural Parade. He asked people to write messages on the canvas. Some of the messages were:

"Let's get rid of the guns."
"Every life is precious."

Sarah Brady, wife of James Brady, is a successful advocate of tighter gun control laws.

"I made it one more year."
"We are the dream, take responsibility."

What Carr is doing is social action. He is using his art to tell people that something should be done about gun violence.

Social action can also be political. Sarah Brady is a powerful political activist for gun control. Since her husband was shot, she has worked for the passage of strict gun laws.

She successfully worked to keep a ban in Maryland on handguns called Saturday Night Specials. Because they are cheap, criminals can easily buy these guns. The NRA spent over 5 million dollars to try to defeat the law, but it failed.

❖ NOT JUST ADULTS ❖

Taking social action is not something only adults can do. Young people of all ages can take action on behalf of society.

When Ross Misher was thirteen years old, his father was killed. He was shot by a man who bought a gun as easily as you could buy a CD. Then he took the gun to work and shot Ross's father.

Because of his father's tragic death, Ross became very active in gun-control efforts. He went to Washington and testified in favor of a "cooling-off period" before anyone could buy a gun.

Throughout high school, Ross worked for gun control in Florida. He wrote to the state legislature, and he founded the Palm Beach County Handgun Control Network. When he went on to college, he started Students Against Handgun Violence.

Ross believes that young people should work to change what is wrong in the world. He believes they can make a difference.

❖ WHY BE AN ACTIVIST? ❖

You are growing up in a time of many problems. Violence is just one of them. Facing so many problems can make people feel hopeless. But you are not alone. People who are concerned about problems in society can work together to change them.

When we feel hopeless, we have two choices. We can do nothing. Or we can work to solve the problem.

Social action can make us feel more hopeful. It lets us take control of a situation that seems out of our control.

Much of the work that activists have done to reduce gun violence has changed gun laws and raised awareness in communities. Sarah Brady tried for several years to get the gun control bill named for her husband to become a law. Her effort helped the Brady Bill to reach Congress and be passed in 1993. Even though it isn't

easy, the work that ordinary people are doing is helping to fight the problem of gun violence.

These people could not ignore the issue because they *care* too much about it. Something inside them wouldn't let them just talk about the problem. They had to do something.

You can do something, too. More and more young people are active in causes now. Adults are listening to them, and they are making a difference.

❖ QUESTIONS TO ASK YOURSELF ❖

People have the power to change things they don't agree with or believe to be dangerous. It takes a lot of work, but it is possible. You might begin thinking about what you can do. 1) What changes would you make regarding the current gun laws? 2) Have you heard about the Toys for Guns program? Gun exchange programs like this will be discussed in chapter eight. Did you know that a teenager suggested the idea to his father, who then implemented it? 3) What projects can you think of to help fight for gun control?

chapter
7
BECOME PART OF THE SOLUTION

In 1993, Colin Ferguson carried a handgun onto a crowded commuter train in New York City. He opened fire, killing six passengers and wounding nineteen others before he was wrestled to the floor and disarmed.

One person whose life was changed by gun violence is Carolyn McCarthy. Her husband was killed and her son was seriously injured in the commuter train attack. After the attack, she gave up her job as a nurse and became an outspoken activist for gun control. She began to lobby Congress for stricter gun control laws. When her own representative in the House of Representatives voted against an assault weapons ban, she decided to run for his seat in Congress—and won. "I am here as a woman with common sense and determination," she said in a speech during her campaign. "And I am going to make a difference."

Many people were shocked to learn about the death of Ennis Cosby, son of actor and comedian Bill Cosby. He was shot while changing a flat tire at the side of a Los Angeles freeway.

❖ RESEARCH ❖

Find out all you can about gun violence and gun control. At the back of this book is a list of other books that would be helpful to read. A librarian can help you to find other books on the subject.

It is also helpful to make lists while you are researching. Write down the names and addresses of organizations, government agencies, and representatives. You can use these lists for surveys and letter-writing.

❖ JOIN FORCES ❖

It's easier if you're not alone. Many of your friends might share your concerns about gun violence. Ask them if they'd like to do something about it. You may be able to turn it into a class project.

Girl or Boy Scout groups or religious youth groups are also good places to get support. Or you can start your own organization as Ross Misher did.

❖ GET OTHER OPINIONS ❖

It's important to find out what other people think about your issue. Research will tell you how much support you have. For instance, you can ask fifty people if they favor gun control. If forty-five people say yes, you know that more people are for it than against it. You can use this information to help persuade other people to support you.

Surveys are good for two reasons: They give you the statistics you need as well as the names of people you can later ask to sign petitions.

For people to take the information seriously, the survey can't be too small or too limited. If your school has ten clubs, you could ask twenty-five people from each one to answer your survey. That way you get lots of different viewpoints.

Survey some adults. Ask ten of your neighbors to participate. Ask your principal if you can survey the teachers at school. You could survey people in the clubs or organizations to which your parents belong.

The more responses you have from the public, the better. Once you start thinking of people to survey, you'll come up with lots of possibilities.

❖ WHAT NOW? ❖

If you have a group that is enthusiastic and organized, there's a lot you can do. We will discuss what you can do as a group in the next chapter.

But if you can't start a group, you still can do things to help. Every effort—big or small—counts. Perhaps all you can do right now is write a few letters.

You can write letters to local or national organizations that are concerned about gun violence to find out what you can do to help. You can also write letters to persuade local and national lawmakers to work against gun violence. You could show support for the actions you agree with, like gun control or stronger penalties for violent criminals.

One student wrote a letter of encouragement to Handgun Control, Inc.

"I am a senior at Plano Senior High School in Texas, and I am concerned about gun violence. I agree with what you are doing, and hope you are successful. Please send me information about your organization. How can I and other teens help?"

You can also write to the people who represent you in Congress. The letter can be as simple as:

Dear . . . .
Too many people die because of guns. I am in favor of strict gun-control laws and would like you to support gun-control bills.

Then sign your name. Include your age and the name of your school.

❖ QUESTIONS TO ASK YOURSELF ❖

The first step toward fighting for gun control is learning as much as you can about the issue. The following questions might help you get started. 1) As public awareness of gun violence has increased, so have the number of articles about the issue in newspapers and various magazines over the last couple of years. How might you get access to these? 2) How can you find out where your local congressional representatives stand on the issue of gun control?

chapter

8

A BLUEPRINT FOR ACTIVISM

THERE ARE SEVERAL WAYS YOU CAN WORK FOR an issue. The first is to raise **awareness**. Speak out about gun violence and gun control. Talk to your friends, your teachers, your parents, your neighbors, anybody who will listen. Let everyone know the seriousness of the issue.

To increase awareness, you can also use the power of the pen. Letters to newspaper editors are a good place to start. (This is a place where you can use some of that research you did.)

The following is part of a very effective letter to an editor. It was written by Arthur Cooper, who lives in Texas.

My seventeen-year-old son died four months ago at the hands of a shooter he didn't know. What in the "old" days would have produced a bloody nose turned into a great loss for our family. All due to the fact that a gun was introduced into the situation.

The grief, shock, and anger felt by those who lose loved ones to gun violence can be channeled into activism.

Let's look at why this letter was so effective. It started with a dramatic illustration of the gun violence problem. Then it got specific. At the time, Texas was considering a law to permit carrying concealed handguns. Arthur Cooper didn't think that law should be passed. To show why, he gave some facts: Texas is one of the most violent states; Texas has more deaths from guns than from auto accidents; guns are the leading cause of death for teenage males.

Then Cooper gave examples of how the law is harmful in other states. Florida allows people to

carry concealed weapons. In February, 1993, people used guns to settle a traffic dispute; two people were killed and two others wounded. In March, 1993, an anti-abortion protestor in Florida shot a doctor.

Cooper ended his letter by asking people to join him in the cause. He had asked the state representatives if they would be influenced by public opinion. They had said they would be. So Cooper told the readers to contact their representatives and let them know if they were against this bill.

❖ POLITICALLY CORRECT ❖

You can also be involved in **lobbying**. This can be done by writing letters and by sending petitions. A petition is usually put together to support or oppose a specific bill.

To find out what bills are being considered, call your state representative. The numbers are listed in the blue pages of the phone book under Government Offices. If you can't find it, ask a teacher or a librarian for help.

When you find a bill you are interested in, find out its exact name and number. Whenever you write or talk about a bill, use its name and number.

Now you can contact the people you surveyed and ask them to write letters. You could even write to clubs in other schools, send a brief statement of the issue, and ask them if they are concerned. Encourage them to write letters to their representatives.

Petitions are also a good way to influence representatives. A petition starts with a brief statement:

> "We the students at (name of school) ask you to support (name and/or number of the bill).
>
> Gun violence kills hundreds of Americans every day. It is the leading cause of death among young people. We believe that this bill is necessary to stop the deaths."

After the statement, provide numbered blank lines for signatures.

Each page of your petition should have the statement at the top. To be most effective, a petition should have 100 or more signatures.

When the petition is complete, make a copy for yourself. Then mail the original to the person you are trying to influence.

❖ IN YOUR COMMUNITY ❖

There are things that you can do about gun violence in your community or school. You can show support for laws that your city, county, or state can pass. There are also events or activities that groups can do to help raise awareness and

Should people today have the right to bear arms?

prevent violence in the areas where you live. You can talk to your school principal or your local police about programs to prevent violence.

One example is a gun exchange. Communities have worked together to reduce the number of guns by allowing people to trade them for merchandise. In Connecticut, local businesses offered up to 500 dollars for each gun that a person gave up to the police. The program, called "Operation Guns for Goods," collected 4,200 guns. In the Washington Heights section of New York City, 1,500 guns were exchanged for toys in a program called "Toys for Guns." Programs like these let the community and the police work together to get guns off the streets.

Young people are learning to resolve conflicts without resorting to violence. You might try to get your school to become one of a growing number that have a peer mediation program. Mediation is a process in which students are able to talk through their disagreements with other people. After schools in Charlotte, North Carolina, tried a mediation program, they found that the number of assaults was cut in half.

❖ **QUESTIONS TO ASK YOURSELF** ❖

Once you decide to take action against gun violence, there are many avenues open to you. How do you decide which to take? Start by considering these questions. 1) Which type of action appeals most to you? 2) Do you feel more comfortable working alone or in groups, such as with a class or a group of friends? 3) What kinds of projects can you work on together?

chapter

9

YOU CAN'T DO IT ALL ALONE

AFTER READING THE LAST CHAPTER, YOU might feel like forgetting the whole idea as being too much work. And you're right. It is too much work for one person.

Now it's time to get organized. Find four or five people who will agree to work with you. Set one specific goal. Maybe you want to support a particular gun-control bill in your state senate. Start making a list of what needs to be done and when.

- Research the bill
- Gather facts about gun violence
- Do surveys and petitions
- Write letters
- Contact other schools and clubs

As you make your list, you will see what needs to be done first. You can't write the letters or make surveys until you have the facts to work with. So it's obvious the research comes first.

Posters, buttons, and pamphlets are some of the tools in an anti-gun campaign.

You don't have to do this part alone either. Get your group together and let everyone be part of the planning.

Once the list is complete, decide who will be responsible for what. As much as possible, match people, talents, and jobs. If Chris is reluctant to talk to more than one person at a time, he wouldn't want to make speeches, but maybe he'd be good at research.

You also need to plan how long some jobs will take. Geri can find out about the bill in a week. But it will take longer for Chris to get the facts about gun violence and gun control.

Meanwhile, someone else can prepare the survey forms. Another person can prepare the petition forms. Someone else can contact other schools and clubs.

Then you will be ready to carry your action through.

Role-play with each other, and practice switching roles, so that you can approach new people with confidence.

You must teach yourselves, and help each other to relax and learn how to get your ideas across to people, without them feeling threatened.

Keep in mind, the first human reaction to new ideas is, "No." That's because it takes the mind a little while to adjust to new thoughts and new ways of looking at problems.

❖ SAMPLE SURVEY FORM ❖

GUN CONTROL SURVEY

SA — strongly agree   A — agree
D — disagree   SD — strongly disagree

1. Gun violence is a serious problem in the United States. . . . . ☐
2. Gun control would help solve the problem . . . . ☐
3. Assault and semiautomatic weapons should be banned . . . . ☐
4. Handguns should be banned . . . . ☐
5. Gun registration and safety training should be mandatory. . . . . ☐
6. Gun buyers should be screened before they buy guns . . . . ☐

This survey is being conducted by

_____

_____

When you get your surveys back, make a record of the answers. A chart will help:

Question #	SA	A	D	SD	Undecided
1	45	25	3	0	10
2	55	20	0	0	9

Make the chart big enough to cover all
the questions and responses.

Make as many pages as you need, all alike.
Number each line for signatures. If you have 20
signatures on the first page, start the second
page numbering at 21, and so on.

❖ SAMPLE PETITION FORM ❖

PETITION FOR GUN CONTROL

To _____
              name of senator or representative

We the undersigned would like to call your
attention to:

_____
              statement of issue

Supported by the following:

1. _____   _____
        name   address/group/school

2. _____   _____
3. _____   _____
4. _____   _____
5. _____   _____
6. _____   _____
7. _____   _____

❖ **SAMPLE SPEECH** ❖

My name is . . . . . and I'm from . . . . (school or group.) Thank you for this opportunity to speak.

I would like to encourage you to support/ oppose . . . .

This is important because . . . . . . (your reasons for supporting or opposing the bill. You can use your petition statement here.)

My stand is based on . . . . . (give the facts that support your position.)

This is a concern that is shared by others . . . . (give the results of your surveys.)

Thank you for your time. I ask for your support.

❖ **QUESTIONS TO ASK YOURSELF** ❖

To be an effective activist, you must be organized. Let's take a look at how you might get organized. 1) What is your strongest argument for (or against) gun control? 2) If you were to write up a list of things to do to accomplish your goals in fighting for gun control, what would it say? 3) How would you divide up the responsibilities on that list?

chapter

10

ORGANIZATIONS CONCERNED ABOUT GUN VIOLENCE

IN WORKING FOR OR AGAINST ANY ISSUE, IT helps to know as much as you can about it. The organizations listed below can provide you with information about gun violence and gun control.

CeaseFire, Inc.
1290 Avenue of the Americas
New York, NY 10104
(212) 484-1616

Citizens Committee for
  the Right to Keep and Bear Arms
12500 NE 10th Place
Bellevue, WA 98005
(206) 454-4911

Coalition to Stop Gun Violence
100 Maryland Avenue, NE
Washington, DC 20002-5625
(202) 530-0340
Web site: http://www.gunfree.org

Handgun Control, Inc.
1225 Eye Street, NW, Suite 1100
Washington, DC 20005
(202) 898-0792

National Rifle Association (NRA)
1600 Rhode Island Avenue, NW
Washington, DC 20036
(202) 828-6000
Web site: http://www.nra.org

Resolving Conflict Creatively Program
National Center
163 Third Avenue #103
New York, NY 10003
(212) 387-0225
e-mail: rccp@igc.apc.org
Web site: www.benjerry.com/esr/index.html

In Canada:
Canadian Firearms Centre
(800) 731-4000
Web site: http://canada.justice.gc.ca/orientations/
    CCAF/index.en.html

Crime Responsibility & Youth
151-10090 152nd Street, Suite 223
Surrey, BC V3R 8X8
(800) CRY-1992
e-mail: cry@deepcove.com
Web site: http://www2.deepcove.com/cry

Whatever your opinion may be, contact people from both sides of the gun control debate. Knowing both sides of an issue helps you to be effective in working for your side. You will be able to make better arguments against the other side of the debate.

Knowing the facts also helps you keep a discussion from becoming a personal attack. When it's not personal, people are more reasonable. If people discuss the problem calmly, we can find solutions that will satisfy most people. We can also find the solutions faster.

❖ QUESTIONS TO ASK YOURSELF ❖

There are many organizations working both for and against gun control. It may be difficult to decide which ones to contact for more information. Answering these questions will help with your decision. 1) Which of the organizations listed work especially with young people?
2) Which group interests you the most and why?

CONCLUSION

Gun violence is a topic that continues to spark much discussion. No one knows what the future holds, but some experts predict that by the year 2003, gun violence will become the leading cause of injury-related death in America. The time to prevent that prediction from becoming a reality is now.

Everybody agrees that gun violence must be stopped. But not everybody agrees on the best way to do it. Some people think that more prisons should be built and more criminals locked up to protect society. Others think that passing tough laws restricting the use of guns is the best solution. No matter what they believe, people are beginning to realize that the problem of gun violence cannot be ignored.

Dedicated groups of people are working to make the epidemic of gun violence a thing of the past. Join them, and you, too, can be part of the solution.

GLOSSARY

assault Violent attack, physical or verbal.

Bill of Rights The first ten amendments to the Constitution.

epidemic Disease or condition that strikes many members of a community at the same time.

homicide The killing of any human being by another.

lobbying Working to influence legislators.

mandatory sentence Punishment that must be given by a judge, if a person is found guilty.

pathologist Scientist who studies the nature of disease and causes of death.

Saturday Night Special Small cheap handgun that is easy to buy on the street.

social scientists People who study human behavior.

statistics Numerical information scientifically gathered and analyzed.

FOR FURTHER READING

Kruschke, Earl R. *Gun Control: A Reference Handbook.* Santa Barbara, CA: ABC-CLIO, 1995.

Lewis, Barbara A. *The Kid's Guide to Social Action.* Minneapolis: Free Spirit Publishing, 1993.

Newton, David E. *Gun Control: An Issue for the Nineties.* Hillside, NJ: Enslow Publishers, 1992.

Nisbet, Lee, ed. *The Gun Control Debate—You Decide.* Buffalo, NY: Prometheus Books, 1990.

Strahinich, Helen. *Think About: Guns in America.* New York: Walker & Company, 1992.

Weksesser, Carol, and Cozik, Charles P. *Gun Control: Current Controversies.* San Diego: Greenhaven Press, 1992.

Winters, Paul A., ed. *Crime and Criminals: Opposing Viewpoints.* San Diego: Greehaven Press, 1995.

Zimring, Franklin E., and Hawkins, Gordon. *The Citizen's Guide to Gun Control.* Greenwich, CT: Macmillan Publishing Company, 1992.

INDEX

ABOUT THE AUTHOR
Maryann Miller has been published in numerous magazines and Dallas newspapers. She has served as editor, columnist, reviewer, and feature writer. Currently she works as an office manager for a book distributor in Dallas.

Married for over twenty-nine years, Ms. Miller is the mother of five children. She and her husband live in Plano, Texas.

PHOTO CREDITS: AP/Wide World Photos, Kim Sonsky/Replay Foundation (p. 7)
PHOTO RESEARCH: Vera Ahmadzadeh
DESIGN: Kim Sonsky